Funny Fish

Written by Cynthia Rider,
based on the original characters
created by Roderick Hunt and Alex Brychta
Illustrated by Alex Brychta

OXFORD
UNIVERSITY PRESS

Mum   Dad   Biff

Chip   Kipper   Floppy

Kipper was fishing.

He got a hat.

Biff was fishing.

She got a crab.

Chip was fishing.

He got an octopus!

Mum was fishing.

She got a bucket.

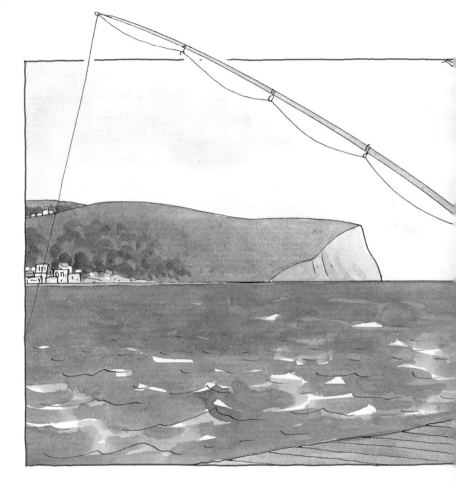

Dad was fishing.

He got a boot.

SPLASH!

Floppy got a fish!

Talk about the story

Why do you think Floppy fell into the water?

Who do you think caught the funniest fish?

What would you do if you caught a big crab, like Biff?

Floppy's fish lives in the sea. Where else do fish live?

Tangled lines

Follow the lines to see who gets the fish.